Original title:
Haiku on a Leaf

Copyright © 2025 Creative Arts Management OÜ
All rights reserved.

Author: Juliana Wentworth
ISBN HARDBACK: 978-1-80566-640-0
ISBN PAPERBACK: 978-1-80566-925-8

Rhythms of Renewal Beneath the Canopy

A leaf plays peek-a-boo,
Fluttering in the sun,
Silly shadows dance along,
Nature's version of fun!

Squirrels chase and tumble by,
Taking turns to trip and fall,
Underneath the laughing trees,
It's a woodland carnival!

Raindrops tap like tiny drums,
Splashing on the lively ground,
Each bounce brings a chuckle forth,
Joy in every droplet found.

As the seasons swirl and twirl,
Leaves burst out in colors bright,
They giggle in the gentle breeze,
What a sight, oh what a sight!

Leaf's Last Embrace

In the breeze, it twirls,
Waving like it's got moves,
Saying goodbye now,
With a final, funny groove.

Falling down, a slow dance,
Trying to hitch a ride,
On a squirrel's big head,
But it missed, what a slide!

Kaleidoscope of Colors

Reds and yellows clash,
A leaf's fashion statement,
Dressing up for fall,
In colors that are blatant.

Spinning down to earth,
Like a twisted confetti,
Stuck in a puddle,
In a leaf-coated jetty.

Echoes in the Shade

Rustling in the wind,
Whispering leaf secrets,
Just like grandma's tales,
Of her favorite pets.

Echoes of a sneeze,
From a guy who walked by,
The leaf giggled loud,
And waved him goodbye.

A Soft Landing on Earth

Plummeting with flair,
It makes a cushy spot,
Right beside a frog,
Who thinks that it's hot.

Frog jumps, leaf flutters,
With a soft, silly spin,
"Catch me if you can!"
But it just won't win!

The Harmony of Withering Grace

In autumn's embrace,
Leaves wear their bright hats.
Flipping down the path,
Making grand splats.

A dance on the breeze,
With giggles with each twist.
Nature's goofy show,
Barely can be missed.

Flickers of Time on Papery Wings

A leaf spins and twirls,
Pretending it's a bird.
Flapping with great flair,
Yet still goes unheard.

Sunbeams chase each hue,
They laugh in bright delight.
But soon get sidetracked,
By shadows of the night.

The Last Waltz of Summer's Kin

With summer's farewell,
Leaves play dress-up in gold.
Each one puts a smile,
   As stories unfold.

A gusty surprise,
They giggle, spin, and dip.
Swirling into dusk,
   On a whim, they flip.

Whirling Wishes on Nature's Canvas

Painting the sky bright,
Leaf-whirls that chase the sun.
But look! What a trick,
   They twirl for fun!

They dream of a ride,
On breezes stout and wide.
Yet land with a thud,
In a laugh, they slide.

Memories Carved in Chlorophyll

A leaf fell from high,
It landed on my sandwich,
Now my lunch is green,
And so is my nose.

The squirrel stole my snack,
With acorns, he is satisfied,
But I want a bite,
Of my chlorophyll treat.

Dancing in the breeze,
Like a ballerina's twirl,
A leaf flirts with clouds,
Waves goodbye to the tree.

In a puddle, it swims,
Trying to be a fish now,
But the rain won't judge,
Just makes it a ship.

Elegy of the Unraveled

Once a leaf so proud,
In summer, it caught the sun,
Now it's a sad brown,
Wishing it was a float.

The winds had their say,
Chasing dreams it couldn't keep,
Oh, the tales it weaves,
Of being a kite once!

Lament, tiny leaf,
For your days of bright glory,
Now you rot in mud,
Next to a lost crayon.

And yet here it lies,
In the yard, a jester still,
A pirate's hat on,
With a rock for treasure.

Whispers of Autumn's Vein

Golden whispers dance,
Amidst rustling, giggling trees,
Each leaf has a tale,
Of long-lost summer days.

Piled high in a heap,
They laugh when kids jump in drops,
Splashes of bright joy,
Nature's confetti rains.

Tickle-me leaves blow,
As they tumble down the path,
A bike swerves for fun,
Avoiding leafy landmines.

In every crisp crunch,
Lies a joke from the old oak,
What did the branch say?
'I'm here for the punchline!'

Dancing Shadows on the Forest Floor

In the forest's dance,
Leaves twirl like ballerinas,
Casting shadows bright,
On the giggling toad.

A leaf took a snooze,
While resting on a frog's back,
Dreamt of flying sky,
But jumped at a fly.

Branches conspire now,
To tickle the moonlit night,
A leaf shimmies soft,
Under the stars' gaze.

Oh, how they all laugh,
With each crinkle and rustle,
The trees throw a bash,
For the colors of fall!

Nature's Pressed Canvas Unfolded

A leaf with a grin,
Snuggled tight in a book,
It dreams of the sun,
And plans its next look.

With colors it flaunts,
Like a fashionista,
Its style, so pronounced,
Grows lighter, but sweeter.

Embracing the Gold of Change

Leaves twirl like dancers,
In a jestful parade,
Golden and rusted,
They laugh unafraid.

Whispers of autumn,
Tickle each branch loud,
"Time to drop, come join!"
They chirp, breezy and proud.

Leaves in the Language of the Breeze

A leaf makes a joke,
As it flutters on by,
Telling the wind,
"I'm too cool to die!"

It giggles and spins,
In its vibrant charade,
"Catch me if you can,
I'm the leaf they parade!"

Fractured Sunshine Against the Bark

Sunlight patches play,
On old rough bark's ground,
The leaves crack a smile,
As laughter resounds.

One says, "I will shine,
In my crooked stance!"
The trees sway along,
In a leafy romance.

An Ode to the Forsaken Shade

Once a glorious green,
Now a crunch underfoot,
Inviting some squirrels,
To dance with delight.

A throne for the ants,
With more royal flair,
While I sip my drink,
On your memory fair.

Wind whispers your tales,
Of sun-soaked bravado,
Now a scrappy joke,
In this warm summer glow.

Yet you crumble, oh friend,
To soil, that's your fate,
In laughter we meet,
Old shade, you're first-rate.

Sunlight's Kiss on a Timeworn Gem

Shining bright and bold,
You're a flawed diamond,
Once the envy of trees,
Now just kindling dreams.

Caught between two branches,
With a shadowy mate,
You twirl in the breeze,
What a silly fate!

Golden rays come down,
For a timid embrace,
Oh, timeworn old gem,
You dance with such grace.

Your colors still shine,
Through laughs and some sighs,
The sun loves your cracks,
You tell no goodbyes.

Secrets of Serenity in the Understory

Under sprawling ferns,
A leaf tells its tales,
Whispers of the wind,
And the chirps of snails.

Sunlight peeks below,
Daring shadows to play,
A giggle escapes,
"Who will win today?"

With a wink it hides,
In this vibrant green,
A comedy show,
Where it's king and queen.

In the cozy dark,
Secrets begin to swell,
A story of laughter,
In the forest's shell.

The Leaf's Story

Once, I was so fresh,
A radiant view,
Tickled by the wind,
With morning's dew.

Now I'm a paper,
In the schoolyard's game,
Flicked by a child's hand,
But I'm not to blame.

My story is funny,
Of heights and free falls,
Of fluttering fun,
In the dance of the squalls.

Though I'm near the end,
My tales still unfold,
In laughter and joy,
I remain very bold.

Ephemeral Dreams of Autumn

A leaf dropped and twirled,
Spinning like a ballerina,
Land with a thud, oh dear!
Nature's comedy club.

Squirrels gather for snacks,
Cornerstone of their diet,
Is this leaf really food?
What a nutty banquet!

Wind confesses a joke,
Tickling branches and trunks,
Leaves giggle, then scatter,
What a raucous farewell!

Autumn's quirky appeal,
Moments like fleeting rain,
With every rustle heard,
A punchline in the breeze.

The Journey of a Tattered Edge

A leaf with frayed edges,
Danced up and down the trail,
Hitching rides with the insects,
That's one wild leaf tale!

Chasing shadows and light,
Falling into a puddle,
Worshipping reflections,
Saying, 'Look at this muddle!'

Caught in the dog's happy bark,
Twirling like a lost kite,
With a flap, it escapes,
'Tis just a leaf's plight.

Tattered, but full of dreams,
Every bend has a story,
Rolling on life's rough waves,
Oh, fleeting leaf glory!

Sunlight Stained Petals

Sunshine splashes on green,
A leaf blushes with glee,
Caught with its friends on grass,
'Can we all take a selfie?'

Rippling laughter echoes,
As shadows pirouette,
"Oh no, don't move too fast,
My filter is a mess!"

Each breeze brings a new joke,
Leaves quibble, then they cheer,
With each flutter they say,
"I'm leafing with good cheer!"

Sunlight, the great artist,
Painting mischief and fun,
In nature's wacky play,
Every petal's a pun.

Secret Stories of the Forest

Whispers in the tall trees,
Leaves gossip as they sway,
"Oh, did you hear that one?"
"Leaf-termination today!"

Mushrooms overhear it all,
With smirks upon their caps,
"Oh, what a tangled web,
In this green mess of laps."

Acorns roll their tiny eyes,
Leaves wobble in great mirth,
'What a wild narrative,
Beneath our forest girth!'

Nature's tales never fade,
In laughter, life we weave,
With each stir and each gust,
The forest's secrets leave!

Skeletons Dressed in Splendor

Bones don their bright attire,
Clothing made of crispy veneer.
Dancing in the autumn breeze,
Bones and leaves twirl with such cheer.

They strut like models on the street,
With every crack, they skip a beat.
Just a spine in golden dress,
In this fashion show, they jest.

Rustling Secrets Beneath the Dome

Whispers of the wind take flight,
Telling tales of leafy night.
What's this rustle, what's the fuss?
An acorn's gossip makes us blush!

Squirrels wear detective hats,
Chasing shadows, zigzag chats.
Who knew beans could spell a plot?
Nature's drama, quite the trot!

Guardian of the Glade's Remains

A tree with glasses and a cane,
Protects the leaves from pesky rain.
Its branches shake like giggling hands,
Warding off those thunder bands.

With bark that wrinkled hides the tales,
Of chipmunks in their tiny sails.
"Hold tight!" it grumbles, wise and craggy,
While squirrels roll by, quite waggly.

A Time Traveler's Portrait of Green

Leaves in a time loop, they conspire,
Painting scenes that never tire.
Back to the days of dandelions,
And carrots wearing leafy lions.

The grapes are laughing in their clutch,
While marigolds gossip as such.
On a cusp of green and gold,
Stories of months they proudly told.

Reflections in the Dew

A leaf in the morn,
Winks at the sun above,
Dew drops hold secrets,
Nature's little love.

A bug takes a sip,
Slips off with a splash,
The leaf laughs aloud,
What a funny crash!

Morning tea for two,
A squirrel joins the chat,
They share silly tales,
Of Sun's big, warm hat.

As daylight drifts on,
The leaf starts to sway,
It dreams of the night,
And the games they'll play.

Transience of the Seasons

A leaf in the breeze,
Twirls like a dancer,
Shouts, 'Look at me go!'
Oh, what a prancer!

Each season it laughs,
At how time likes to tease,
Falling with a plop,
Just taking it easy.

Spring wears a bright crown,
While summer brings heat,
But autumn arrives,
And it can't feel its feet!

Winter, cold and clear,
Whispers a silly cheer,
'I'll catch you next time,
When the frost disappears!'

A Rustic Tapestry Unfolded

In the woods it gleams,
A tapestry bright,
The leaves weave a tale,
Of the day and the night.

A leaf draped in gold,
Jokes with a pine cone,
'You're pretty prickly,
Why don't you just roam?'

They chuckle at clouds,
And rain's funny drip,
All nature's a stage,
Join in on the trip!

With each rustling sound,
An applause from the trees,
They all play their parts,
In the wind's gentle breeze.

The Sound of Rustling Silence

A leaf whispers soft,
In the still morning light,
'Listen to my tales,
They tickle the night!'

Each rustle, a laugh,
At the spider's fine web,
'How did you get here?
You've got quite the ebb!'

The wind joins the fun,
Swirling all around,
Each chuckle and cheer,
A harmonious sound.

When silence takes hold,
And the day starts to fade,
A leaf fills the air,
With joy never staid.

Underneath

Underneath the boughs,
Squirrels plot their schemes,
Chasing after acorns,
Unraveling their dreams.

A sneaky little crow,
Barges in for a snack,
Raucous laughter echoed,
Nature's own hijack.

The grass grows like a wild rug,
Tickling toes in mirth,
Where playful chaos reigns,
And fun has endless worth.

Stories of Seasons Past

Whispers of the past,
Leaves chortle on the breeze,
They giggle tales of days,
When summers aimed to tease.

Autumn sipped its cider,
While winter took a nap,
Spring donned a flower crown,
Then tripped upon a flap.

A leaf began to tumble,
Into a puddle's prank,
With splashes of confusion,
They formed a leafy bank.

Watercolors of the Wind's Embrace

In the wind's delight,
Colors swirl and twirl,
Pinks, greens, and golds dance,
As nature's rags unfurl.

A leaf chose a spin,
To make a grand entry,
But ended with a flop,
Now part of history!

With brushes made of breezes,
The sky's a canvas wide,
Each laugh holds a stroke,
As daylight opens wide.

The Dance of Light on Fragile Edges

A glint of sunlight plays,
On edges thin and bright,
Leaves shimmy in the glow,
In a whimsical flight.

A shadow makes a move,
To join the silly jive,
While a beetle taps a beat,
To keep the fun alive.

In a giggly waltz,
The leaves sway and sway,
Forgotten are the storms,
In this dance of play.

Cadence of Colors in Twilight's Grip

Twilight hums a tune,
With hues that never cease,
Leaves chuckle gently,
In perfect, silly peace.

Underneath the brush,
A raccoon dons a hat,
A leaf wants to join in,
But now it's gone flat!

With colors fading fast,
They make a funny scene,
Twilight's laugh resounds,
In a shade-rich routine.

Fading Echoes of a Green Tapestry

Once a bright green swatch,
Now a crinkled crouton,
With a dance of the breeze,
It flops like a floppy hat.

In the fall's raucous laughter,
Colors scatter and spin,
A leaf's vibrant tale,
Now a comedy of air.

The Soft Touch of Evening's Gait

When the sun loses grip,
A leaf trips over shadows,
Wearing dusk like a cloak,
Stumbling in a starry breeze.

A tickle from the branches,
Giggles of sway and swirl,
A soft, fluttering dance,
To a tune of twinkling times.

Rustling Remnants of a Swirling Past

A once-bold green rebel,
Now just a paperweight,
With stories spun in whirlwind,
Of a fork in the air less traveled.

The ground holds its punchlines,
Tickling toes with a crunch,
In the chaos of colors,
Every crinkle sings a joke.

The Diary of Seasons Lifted by the Wind

Chronicles written thin,
Each page a breezy tumble,
Winds read the secrets,
Of a leaf with too much sass.

Unexpectedly airborne,
The leaf flips through its past,
In giggles of gusty pages,
Scribbles of laughter unbound.

Silent Sagas in the Woodland

In the breeze, they flutter,
Whispering tales of yore,
Acorns play hide and seek,
While squirrels snatch them more.

A leaf once danced on air,
But took a slip and fell,
Landed on a sleeping dog,
Now they share a tale to tell.

Rooted trees roll their eyes,
As chatter fills the glade,
Oh, the gossiping grasses,
Spreading rumors, unafraid.

Nature's chuckle echoes,
In every rustling sound,
And the mischief of the leaves,
Keeps the woodland laughter bound.

Nature's Lyrical Farewell

Leaves are waving goodbye,
In their swaying ballet,
One twirls over a puddle,
Creating splashes all day.

The branches start to tease,
As the colors begin to shift,
"Is that your winter coat?"
Said the wind with a gift.

With a wink, the sun dips low,
Turning gold into rust,
A leaf takes one last twirl,
And lands in the dust.

Their party is a riot,
A feast of autumn cheer,
The Earth holds its belly,
And giggles, "What a year!"

The Tapestry of Seasons Aflame

Autumn leaves like confetti,
Twirling down with style,
A leaf with flair, no doubt,
Said, "Watch me, stay awhile!"

They gossip about the frost,
As winter moves in fast,
One leaf thinks it's a race,
"I must outlast the blast!"

Colors clash in wild hues,
Nature's art gets quite loud,
While a leaf jokingly shouts,
"Can someone call a crowd?"

As they settle, quiet now,
Wrapped in their vibrant beds,
Nature sighs, chuckles low,
"What a show, those leafy heads!"

A Solitary Dance of Decay

One leaf on a solo flight,
Spins like a dancer bold,
But trip on a twig it might,
And land—not in the gold.

With each sway through the air,
It shouts, "Look at my flair!"
Until it finds the ground,
Then it laughs, unaware.

A worm pops up and says,
"Hey, that's quite the stunt!
But don't you think you'll stick
Where the mushrooms have a front?"

And as twilight enchants,
The leaves play tag with dusk,
Decay might seem quite grim,
Yet, oh, it's truly a fuss!

The Quiet Farewell of the Bold

A fierce green warrior,
Dares to drop from his perch,
"Catch me if you can!"
He swirls in the crisp air.

He lands on a hungry frog,
Who blinks with surprise now,
A leaf-flavored snack,
'Til it croaks in despair.

The wind giggles softly,
Tickling branches awake,
A dance of the silly,
As chaos starts to reign.

With every gust they sway,
The brave ones spiral down,
A fluttered brigade,
Creating giggly sounds.

Veil of Enchantment Draped in Gold

A golden leaf prances,
Dressed in sunshine's embrace,
"Look at my fine gown!"
It twirls with starry grace.

A squirrel gives a wink,
"You've got the moves, my friend!"
With a leap and a dash,
Forest parties never end.

The sunlight plays peek-a-boo,
With shadows on the ground,
Each flutter's a party,
In nature's playground found.

"Let's dance until we fade!"
Cried the leaf with great cheer,
Then down it went spinning,
In a stage of applause clear.

Shimmers of Resilience in the Forest

A crinkled old leaf sighs,
Bragging of battles fought,
"I'm still here," it boasts,
While clinging to its spot.

The owls hoot in laughter,
As breezes pull and tease,
"Hold on, you old trooper!
This isn't time for ease!"

With each gust it chuckles,
Finding strength in its plight,
A true forest hero,
In the shimmering light.

Its stories are scattered,
On the ground, vague and sweet,
Like whispers of laughter,
In a world so complete.

Fluttering Fables of the Verdant Realm

A leaf penned a tale,
In a flutter, it swirled,
"Once I was a tree,"
In the great leafy world.

It told of the seasons,
And the friends that it made,
The naughty little bugs,
That stole beauty and shade.

With every windy twist,
The stories danced alive,
Friends giggled and swayed,
In the wind, they would thrive.

"Gather 'round," it beckons,
"Let's share a wild spree,"
The forest bursts with giggles,
In the grand leafy jubilee!

Whispers of the Canopy

Leaves giggle softly,
Swinging on branches high,
Squirrels gossip wildly,
While birds just fly by.

A leaf sneezes loudly,
Causing a flutter,
The wind starts to dance,
As trees fill with clutter.

Sunshine tickles trunks,
While shadows play hide,
Nature's playful prank,
Calls laughter inside.

With each rustle near,
Jokes fly through the air,
A canopy's cheer,
Paints smiles everywhere.

Dancer in the Breeze

A leaf takes a twirl,
In a comical whirl,
Spinning round and round,
Like it's in a swirl.

Dancing with the gusts,
It wobbles and dips,
Then takes a big leap,
And flaps like it's flipping.

With each flip and flop,
It sends giggles wide,
Making plants laugh too,
As they sway with pride.

Soon it lands on grass,
Breathless from its spree,
The forest claps hands,
'Bravo for the free!'

A Single Green Flutter

One leaf waved at me,
With a wink and a grin,
'Catch me if you can,'
It dared me to begin.

Up high on a branch,
It jiggled with glee,
'Round and round we go!',
It laughed, 'Just try to see!'

A chase ensued fast,
As I tripped on air,
The leaf just giggled,
From its lofty chair.

Finally it landed,
Right on my small hat,
'This dance is so sweet,'
I laughed, 'I like that!'

Nature's Quiet Palette

In hues of bright green,
Leaves come out to play,
Splashing joy around,
In a splendid way.

A paintbrush of winds,
Swirls colors about,
Strokes whispers of fun,
In the sunshine's shout.

Each flicker and bend,
Creates strange shapes anew,
A gallery blooms,
In the morning dew.

As night brings a hush,
The leaves softly snore,
Their artistry slumbers,
Until the day's roar.

Tides of Time in Green

In the breeze we sway,
Juggling colors like clowns,
Nature's funny show,
Tickling the air, we laugh.

The sun drops like candy,
On this tree's sticky hands.
Squirrels plan their pranks,
While we cheer from above.

Leaves dance in two-step,
Whispering jokes to the sky.
Laughter fills the woods,
As shadows play tag below.

Oh, what a comedy,
Each rustle a punchline.
Nature's giddy play,
With every leaf a grin.

The Language of Loss

When a leaf drops down,
It doesn't say goodbye.
Instead, it whispers,
"I'll be back - just hang tight!"

A funny little dance,
Spinning through the cool air.
No tears, just a giggle,
As they spin on a whim.

Branches tell tall tales,
Of leaves that flew too high.
Comical goodbyes,
In a playful breeze way.

Lost but still around,
Each flake of color grins.
Nature's way of jest,
In the cycle of fun.

Veins of the Earth

Roots wiggle like worms,
In a game of hide and seek.
Laughter underground,
As branches trade their hues.

The earth is quite sly,
With its jokes buried deep.
Every vein a quip,
Tickling grass and soil.

Overhead, leaves greet,
In a chorus of chuckles.
Telling secrets,
Where the microbes dance free.

So gather round this chat,
Join the chorus, my friend.
For in every root,
Lies a punchline of green.

Conversations with the Wind

Oh, how the wind jokes,
Twirling leaves in a twist.
Each gust a new laugh,
As branches bend with glee.

"Watch out for the pollen!"
The leaves giggle and sneeze.
Nature's immuno-fun,
A tickle in the breeze.

Quirky whispers fly,
Through the forest at play.
Nature's secret chat,
Soaring high in the air.

Listen to the jokes,
The rustle tells it all.
The wind, it never tires,
As laughter swirls around.

Tread Lightly on Nature's Memory Lane

A leaf fell on my hat,
I tipped it with a grin.
Nature's little prankster
Reminds me where I've been.

I stealthily step through
The crunch of memories.
Each crackle recalls stories,
From antics of the bees.

I chase a wayward breeze,
It tickles my bare toes.
The leaf laughs as it swirls,
We share our little woes.

In this whimsical waltz,
I dance among the blooms.
Nature, you clever jester,
Play tricks in garden rooms.

Brushstrokes of Wind Against the Sky

A cloud of fluff drifts by,
I catch it in my hand.
It giggles, takes a flight,
Leaving me, leaf in hand.

The wind cracks silly jokes,
It tickles every bough.
I laugh beneath the trees,
Join in the fun somehow.

Colors splash like paint
Across the bending grass.
A leaf waves mockingly,
'Can you keep up, you ass?'

Painted whispers of breeze
Encourage me to play.
Shall I giggle with the leaves?
Let's dance the day away!

Thoughts Scribbled in Vibrant Deco

On a leaf, I scribbled,
My dreams in bright crayon.
The world paused for a moment,
And then, the wind was gone.

Birds cawed at my canvas,
They squawked like a mean boss.
I tried to shoo them off,
But they laughed; I was the loss.

A squirrel made a sketch,
With nuts on my design.
'Is this art?' I pondered,
'Or just his lunch combined?'

So I laughed at nature,
And my mixing of the hues.
For in this wild gallery,
There're many kinds of views.

The Dance of Nature's Fertile Soul

A leaf spins 'round and round,
It's waltzing on the breeze.
'Can you dance?' it teases me,
So I shimmy with some trees.

The flowers join in fast,
They bop and sway with glee.
Even grumpy old oaks,
Are swaying, can't you see?

In this grand jubilee,
We prance on ground of green.
I ask the frog for tips,
'It's all in the unseen.'

Nature's dance of life
Is filled with quirky fun.
When the music of the leaf
Sings, we all become one!

Timeless Truths in Crispy Corners

A leaf in my lunch,
Whispers tales of the tree,
Daring to jump high,
It flutters with glee.

Munching on its edges,
Crunchy tales to be told,
Wishing for a breeze,
To dance with the bold.

Brocade of Earth and Sky

Colors in chaos,
An artist's palette falls,
A leaf blinks awake,
It giggles and sprawls.

Drifting on the ground,
It plays hide and seek,
Catching little ants,
With a playful peek.

A Journey Through Time's Gentle Caress

Rotting leaves in piles,
An autumn's great prank,
Sitting on the porch,
With a leaf as my flank.

Time tickles my nose,
As I shuffle and sway,
This leaf starts to laugh,
And rolls right away!

Lyrical Dreams in Shades of Decay

A leaf fell today,
Dramatic with flair,
It spun like a star,
In the crisp autumn air.

It landed on a shoe,
And screamed, "What a catch!"
But with a swift kick,
It learned it's not that!

Celestial Whispers on Fragile Wings

A leaf took a trip,
To the moon for a glance,
Came back with a scoop,
Of stars in its dance.

It tickled the breeze,
And swirled in a spin,
Said, "Look at me shine!"
"I'm a star in the skin!"

The ants held a feast,
For a leaf in full flight,
They danced in a line,
Claiming victory in sight.

A gust made it whine,
With a fluttering shout,
"Do trees hear me now?"
"I'm more than just sprout!"

Tapestries Tangled in Nature's Whim

In a tangle of green,
A leaf had a chat,
With a snail in a shell,
"You look like a brat!"

They laughed at the sun,
Who tried to be bright,
While the clouds played hide,
In a game of kite.

The squirrel wore it proud,
As a hat on his head,
Declared, "I am trendy!"
And then off he sped.

A ladybug danced,
On its paper-like skin,
Said, "Join me my friend,
Let the giggles begin!"

Lost Chronicles in the Forest's Embrace

Once a leaf wrote tales,
About squirrels so sly,
Who tried to outsmart,
A crow in the sky.

With ink made of dew,
And a pen from a twig,
Its stories would twirl,
Like a jig in a gig.

But the wind was a thief,
On a mischievous run,
Took the tales for a ride,
Said, "I'm just having fun!"

Now the forest reads,
The tales on the breeze,
A comedy show,
In the rustling trees.

Timeworn Letters from Ol' Green

Ol' Green wrote a note,
To the branch by his side,
"You're looking quite spry,
But I've got more pride!"

With a flap and a flap,
He sent it with glee,
The bird took the chance,
And dropped it on me!

Now I'm reading the lore,
Of leaves in a chat,
The gossip of roots,
With whispers of flat.

Laughter cascades down,
From the trees to the ground,
As timeworn old letters,
In the breeze are found.

The Poetry of Silence Wrapped in Green

In the breeze, it twirls,
A leaf with dreams of flight,
But hangs on tight, just shy,
Oh, to be a bird tonight!

It giggles in the wind,
Teasing branches, swaying low,
Daring gravity to play,
"Catch me if you can, oh no!"

Sunbeams dance upon its face,
While shadows play hide and seek,
It flips and flops, a merry race,
Nature's jester, oh so cheek!

When the rains begin to pour,
It wears a hat of droplets,
Sips the puddles by the shore,
And laughs at all the soggy pets!

A Symphony Played by Nature's Breath

A leaf on stage does prance,
Conducted by the gentle breeze,
Rustling notes, a curious dance,
Tickles nerves, puts minds at ease.

With every flap, it sings along,
An orchestra of green delight,
But oh, it trips, such comic wrong,
A tumble into morning light!

Still it sways, a merry band,
Puddles echo its sweet cheer,
Nature's humor, grand and grand,
Leaves us chuckling ear to ear!

When autumn comes with grand applause,
It blushes bright in vivid hue,
Then takes a bow—what a cause!
As winds bid it a fond adieu!

The Last Flicker Before Stillness

A leaf, a flicker, then a sway,
It bids farewell with style and grace,
Performing acrobatics today,
While all the rest just hold their place.

In a final twist, it spins around,
Practicing its great escape,
Then flutters down to grassy ground,
Leaving dreams of citrus shape.

Among the blades, it finds a spot,
A resting place, both soft and neat,
With whispers low, it gives a thought,
"I miss that breeze beneath my feet!"

Suddenly, a ladybug stops by,
To share a joke and laugh a beat,
And for that moment, they both fly,
In the warmth of nature's greet!

Chronicles of Change in Robust Colors

Once vibrant green, it now turns gold,
Telling tales of time once bright,
A leaf with stories yet untold,
It glimmers in the autumn light.

With every change, it does proclaim,
"Watch me sparkle in the fall!"
A humorist in nature's game,
It chuckles, dances, having a ball!

Beneath the tree, the stories spread,
A legend of the seasons' spin,
As squirrels chatter overhead,
Planning mischief, where to begin!

And when at last it hits the ground,
It makes a crunch, a funny sound,
Nature's laughter all around,
With every leaf, a jester crowned!

Petals of Breath and Dreams

A leaf sneezes bright,
Spreading pollen like jokes,
Laughter fills the air,
Nature's playful surprise.

Swinging in the breeze,
Whispers turn to giggles,
Sunlight tickles green,
Trees join in their joy.

A tiny bug dances,
On its stage of chlorophyll,
Audience of clouds,
Cheering with soft rain.

As shadows start to creep,
The leaf plays hide and seek,
Each rustle a giggle,
Nature's comedy show.

Voyage of the Woodland's Last Breath

In the breeze, a sigh,
A leaf takes its last trip,
Suitcase made of green,
Adventure calls it forth.

Frogs watch from the pond,
As it flutters and lands,
A silly goodbye,
From the height of a branch.

On a mossy pillow,
The leaf tells its wild tales,
Of windswept travels,
And squirrels with big hats.

Forgotten by the tree,
The leaf waits for a friend,
Bugs gather 'round,
Storytime begins now.

Inked Aria of the Earth's Pages

A leaf dreams in ink,
Writing down its secrets,
With rain as the pen,
And sun for the bright hue.

It scrolls through the sky,
Signing autographs with jets,
A plane waves hello,
As the leaf shares its verse.

Falling with a twist,
It plays tag with the wind's laugh,
Scribbles in the air,
Art that flows and twirls.

In a puddle's mirror,
Reflecting brush strokes of life,
The world in full bloom,
A masterpiece of fun.

The Essence of Time in a Leaf's Fold

A leaf folded laughs,
Time trapped in its green veins,
Tick-tock of the breeze,
Nature's calendar rolls.

Caught in a gust's hand,
It swirls in a dizzy dance,
Time does the cha-cha,
With shadows playing along.

Between folds of laughter,
The past whispers sweet tales,
Of sunlit mornings,
And moonlit evenings bright.

When autumn rolls in,
Colors burst with a giggle,
Each rustle a quip,
As time keeps spinning round.

A Whispered Breath Among the Boughs

A leaf flipped its hat,
Giggled like a silly cat.
Chasing winds with flair,
Its dance a comical affair.

Beneath the sky so wide,
A twig plays hide and seek,
It pokes the lazy clouds,
And whispers secrets so meek.

Sunbeams tickle its veins,
Making shadows clap in glee,
As the breeze cracks a joke,
Oh, such a sight to see!

Each rustle holds a giggle,
An emerald chuckle's tease,
In the silliness of nature,
Joy dances on the breeze.

Fluttering Memories on the Wind

Round and round they twirl,
Leaves like confetti swirl.
Each gust a playful nudge,
In a leafy little grudge.

Old friends from the tree,
Short-lived but oh so spry,
They make a raucous scene,
As they bid the earth goodbye.

Landed on a puppy's nose,
With a wag, it does propose,
To chase and chew and play,
Leafy laughter on display.

Memories swirl in gain,
As the wind writes tales anew,
Silly voices echo loud,
In the cackle of the view.

Echoes of Green in Time's Tidal Flow

Time races like a hare,
Leaves tumble without a care.
They laugh on fallen ground,
Found in whispers all around.

Tickling the frowning grass,
As they hide and seek with sass.
Nature's fair comedic spree,
While the world just grins with glee.

Each twist a giggling sigh,
Bouncing 'neath the lazy sky.
A leaf's confession made,
Of how laughter's never spayed.

Echoes dance with careless ease,
In the laughter of the trees,
For in every flip and flap,
Life's humor takes a nap.